What's the Deal with Bitcoins?

by

Ryan Lancelot and Jack Tatar

What's the Deal with Bitcoins?
ISBN-10:0985082062
ISBN-13:978-0-9850820-6-2

Library of Congress Cataloging-in-Publication Data is available upon request.

Published by PeopleTested® Publications
www.PeopleTested.com

Table of Contents

Bitcoin: A Tulip or a Financial Tool?

By now, with all of its recent fervor, you have undoubtedly heard about Bitcoin, the completely digital currency that has found investors rethinking their portfolios. Though some have found Bitcoin to be a fascinating new venture and an original way to look at currency, many others can't help but think about tulips.

Tulips? Yes, tulips. These flowers are commonly used to reference an age old economic phenomenon that occurred in the early 1600s in the Netherlands. The 17th century found the Netherlands a newly independent country with an economy built upon booming trade. Dutch merchants sailed from the East Indies touting all manners of foreign delicacies and trinkets, and fetched high prices for their wares.[1]

One such curiosity brought back from the eastern trade routes was the tulip, a colorful flower that, at this time in

1 Tulipomania. Grout, James. Encyclopaedia Romana, http://penelope.uchicago.edu/~grout/encyclopaedia_romana/aconite/tulipomania.html

European history, was a wonder to horticulturalists. The flower exhibited properties entirely disparate from the known plants of the western world. It had colors more intense and varying than any other flower and could withstand the harsh climate of the Netherlands. Because of these qualities and the limited supply of their seeds, the acquisition of tulips became a very lucrative prospect. In the 1630s, the tulip trade built into mania and its bulbs were being traded for enormous sums of money because of the perceived value of the flowers by both enthusiasts and speculators alike.[2]

As with any other kind of "bubble", as we would call this type of economic situation today, demand for tulip bulbs rapidly outpaced the flower's actual supply. Whenever this happens, the price of the good is artificially inflated to exorbitant levels. As has been exhibited countless times throughout history, goods commanding perceived value can only sustain such ridiculous price levels for so long until the demand bubble bursts. The tulip bubble did finally burst largely because, after all, tulips are only flowers. In this way, the mention of tulip mania has become synonymous with the folly of speculative investors who get caught up in the hype of a novelty investment.[3]

Returning to Bitcoin, the question may be is this digital currency one big, bursting tulip? But before jumping to conclusions, we need to learn more about Bitcoin.

---

2 Tulip Mania. (n.d.). In *Wikipedia.* Retrieved May 7, 2013, from http://en.wikipedia.org/wiki/Tulip_mania

3 When the Tulip Bubble Burst. Frankel, Mark. from "Tulipomania The Story of the World's most Coveted Flower," Dash, Mark. http://www.businessweek.com/2000/00_17/b3678084.htm

Purpose of this Book

The purpose of this book is to inform those new to Bitcoin of its merits as a digital currency and how this financial phenomenon can be used to make money. Much of the beginning of this book will be an explanation of the ins and outs of Bitcoin. For those wishing to skip the details of the mechanics of Bitcoin, please note that without a complete understanding of what Bitcoin is and how it functions, it will be difficult to understand how it's possible to build wealth with the currency. Because of this, it is recommended that readers take more than a passing glance at those sections of the book before proceeding onward.

Another point worth noting is that this book does not outline a "get rich quick" scheme. While the concept of Bitcoin may seem gimmicky, in truth, the currency functions in the real world as a mechanism to transfer value between parties, much the same as the dollar functions in online transactions. Keep in mind that this book will not seek to undermine Bitcoin from its purpose as an online currency for the sake of profit. In fact, only by propagating the use of Bitcoin will the methods within this book prove lucrative. With these things in mind, keep an open mind.

History will ultimately bear out if Bitcoins are a success or not. This book will help you to become knowledgeable enough about them to not only understand them, but to have an opinion on how they may impact you as well.

What are Bitcoins?

Bitcoin is, at its core, virtual currency. It is a digital representation of money that can be used to purchase goods and services in the same way cash can be used to purchase those same goods and services. In this sense it is similar to the dollar, Euro, Peso, or any other type of printed currency. However, Bitcoin differs considerably from these other currencies in that it is not backed by any bank or nation and has no formal organizational structure behind it. Instead, Bitcoin is managed entirely by a Peer to Peer (P2P) network of individuals that manages balances and transactions on its own.[4]

The Bitcoin concept was first circulated in 2009 by an unknown individual on a Cryptography mailing list who used the pseudonym Satoshi Nakamoto. This individual based Bitcoin on the concept of crypto-currency and designed Bitcoin to use cryptography to control the creation and operation of this new currency. The goal was to provide the world with an alternative currency that existed for the purpose of online transactions. While PayPal and its ilk exist and function today,

---

4 About Bitcoin. Buterin Vitalik. © Bitcoin Project 2009–2013 Released under the MIT license, http://bitcoin.org/en/about

they still have a currency impediment when transactions occur across borders. Bitcoin seeks to address that issue by allowing Bitcoin holders to transact with a common currency in an increasingly global marketplace. With this new digital currency, someone in Britain can buy a book from someone in Boston without many of the fees a bank would surely place on this transaction.[5]

Steadily, Bitcoin's P2P network has developed the project to its current iteration, gaining notoriety and media attention for its conceptual merits. In September of 2012, the Bitcoin Foundation formed to help regulate the currency and its continued improvement. As of this writing, its current circulation is roughly 13.5 million Bitcoins worth approximately $1.8 billion. These big numbers are indicative of the large scale interest Bitcoin is gaining. People are intrigued by the way Bitcoin works and what's more is that it actually works as a means of online payment.[5]

How Do They Work?

In order to create a digital currency with no centralized organization behind transactions, Bitcoin was designed in such a way that users themselves actually verify and complete transactions. This is made possible through Bitcoin's Blockchain. The blockchain is essentially a public chronological log of every confirmed transaction that occurs between Bitcoin addresses. Using cryptography Bitcoin creates mathematical proofs to secure the blockchain and safeguard users' transactions. These proofs are verified by users who process the blocks that are part of the blockchain by "mining". Users mine

5 The Rise and Fall of Bitcoin. Wallce, Benjamin. Wired.com © 2013. All rights reserved. http://www.wired.com/magazine/2011/11/mf_bitcoin/all

through the use of software that endlessly attempts to solve the complex mathematical proofs securing the blockchain. This allows the system to transmit transactions to the network almost immediately and verify them within the hour. Because mining assists in the creation of the ledger of payments with Bitcoins, it helps to ensure that double spending, or a user's attempt to send the same Bitcoins to two people at once, is prevented. In this way, users contribute directly to Bitcoin, supporting the currency's well being. However, transaction processing and strengthening security are not the only purposes of mining.[6]

Before delving into these alternate purposes, something may be nagging at you about this setup. Having users mine these mathematical proofs is what allows Bitcoin to function without a bank or some other type of transactional middle man, but why would users verify transactions with no incentive? It's safe to say that no one would drop what they were doing to assist their local bank branch with processing their clients' transactions for free. It would be an unreasonable suggestion. Similarly, contributing to the Bitcoin community is certainly rewarding, but mining takes considerable processing power by computers which results in the expenditure of time and energy that most users wouldn't want to just give away. As it turns out, this computing power is not being exhausted for naught but goodwill. For every block processed miners are rewarded with the creation of new Bitcoins. Mining, therefore, is a means to obtaining more Bitcoins for currency holders.[7]

6 How Does Bitcoin Work? Buterin Vitalik. © Bitcoin Project 2009–2013 Released under the MIT license, http://bitcoin.org/en/how-it-works

7 A guide to Bitcoin Mining: Why Someone bought a $1500 Bitcoin Miner for $20,600. Liu, Alec. http://motherboard.vice.com/blog/a-guide-to-bitcoin-mining-why-someone-bought-a-1500-bitcoin-miner-on-ebay-for-20600

It is important to understand that mining for Bitcoins is not an entirely self serving process with platform maintenance as a side effect. While it does lead to the personal gain of Bitcoins for the individuals who successfully mine the block, these individuals are simultaneously helping the system distribute wealth evenly and fairly among its user base. Bitcoin is designed so that mining has diminishing returns on multiple levels for this very reason. Currently, the reward per block processed is 25 Bitcoins. This is a step down from November of 2012 when the previous reward per block processed was 50 Bitcoins. In 2017, the reward will be reduced further to 12.5 Bitcoins.

The reason for this gradual decline in rewards is due in part because there are a limited number of Bitcoins that will ever be in existence, roughly 21 million. In order to maintain the value of the Bitcoin, as time goes on and more Bitcoins are mined and introduced into the global marketplace, it must become increasingly difficult to obtain one. Other ways the system achieves this is by ensuring that there is a steady increase in the difficulty of the mathematical equations of each block introduced, and by regulating the number of solutions found by miners over time. Now, because every 4 years the number of Bitcoins rewarded for processing a block has halved and the complexity of the mathematical equations has increased significantly since the currency's creation, mining has become an expensive affair.

At this point in the Bitcoin mining cycle it has become virtually impossible to compute the amount of information necessary to process a block as an individual without incurring tremendous hardware and energy costs. Thus, the Bitcoin community has taken to creating pools to merge resources and more effectively mine for the currency. That said, the most important takeaway about mining at the moment is that it not only creates new Bitcoins but also helps process transactions, secure the network, and allows the system to distribute wealth in as fair a manner as possible.[8]

Mining is one way to obtain Bitcoins, but, as previously mentioned, mining will likely not prove as fruitful as it once was. Because of this, most people currently obtain Bitcoins either by purchasing them, or offering some good or service that entices someone to pay for that good or service in Bitcoins. However, neither of these can be done without an electronic wallet. The purely digital nature of Bitcoins does not allow for more familiar means of storing currency. There's no way to take it out of the system and put it under the mattress. The only way to actually become a holder of this currency is to acquire an electronic wallet.

As of this writing there are multiple electronic wallet providers to choose from such as Bitcoin-QT, Multibit, Armory, and Electrum. There are mobile and web based wallets available as well. These providers will give users the ability to store their Bitcoins and send them wherever they like. This is done by providing users with a secure Bitcoin address that can be further encrypted with a password to safeguard against hacking attempts. For anyone just starting out with Bitcoin, there are several essential things that they need to know about actually owning Bitcoins. Because of the way the system was designed, the Bitcoins that are held by users cannot be claimed by anyone but the user. Governments can confiscate their currencies from individuals for a variety of reasons, but with Bitcoin, only the individual or individuals who

8 Pooled Mining. Bitcoin Wiki. Retrieved May 7,2013, from https://en.bitcoin.it/wiki/Pooled_mining

know both the address and password of a wallet can utilize the currency inside of it. The upside of this feature is that no Bitcoin can be seized or frozen. Bitcoins are either in a wallet or they are not, and able to be used or not. In this way, Bitcoin is a great boon for those looking to secure assets. However, this can potentially be a problem if a user forgets his/her address, password, or both. If this is the case, because there is no way to recover the password, the Bitcoins are lost not only to the user, but to the entire network.[9]

Another similar concern due to the electronic nature of Bitcoin is that the wallets themselves are only as secure as the provider can make them. Individuals' wallets are dependent on the security of the wallet providers in the event of some kind of incident on their part. If a provider shuts down its services, all of the Bitcoins within the wallets it secures that are not backed up will effectively vanish from the network. With this in mind, it is of extreme importance for all new users to take measures to ensure that their passwords and wallets are protected and backed up somewhere, preferably offline. Passwords can be written down and put away easily enough or saved in a word processing document on a computer. Wallets can be made safe by placing copies onto external storage devices, like USB flash drives, and safeguarding these now, slightly more physical copies. Not only will this protect you in case of some grand failure by a wallet provider, as was the case with the Mt. Gox exchange, but it will secure your Bitcoins in case of computer trouble.[9]

Actually utilizing Bitcoin is similar to any other online payment system. An easy way to describe it would be like PayPal

9 Some Things you need to know. Buterin, Vitalik. © Bitcoin Project 2009–2013 Released under the MIT license, http://bitcoin.org/en/you-need-to-know

but with its own, separate currency. Users' wallets show how many Bitcoins they currently own as well as recent transactions both pending and verified. Bitcoins may be transferred between Bitcoin holders on any node throughout the world. Bitcoins allow for a transfer of the currency anywhere for any offered good or service. An example of this would be if a Bitcoin user was interested in creating his/her own website and utilized Wordpress to do so. If, hypothetically, he/she was unsatisfied by the free version of the program, instead of purchasing an upgrade with dollars through PayPal, he/she would be able to pay with Bitcoins. A more practical example may be provided by a bar in New York City that announced that its patrons may pay for their food and drink with Bitcoins. If a Bitcoin holder goes into the bar, he/she can use a Bitcoin payment app on a smart phone to pay for the consumed indulgences.[10]

Something that should be noted is that the transfer of Bitcoins is an irreversible transaction. Once Bitcoins are sent to another user, they cannot be refunded as they could be when using a credit card. This is one of the negatives of using Bitcoins. The lack of a central institution such as a bank cannot intervene on your behalf to dispute the transaction if Bitcoins were mistakenly sent to a user. That said, while Bitcoin transactions are irreversible, a request can be made to the individual to whom the Bitcoins were mistakenly sent. The individual could be urged to send that same amount back, and under most circumstances he/she would be glad to do so. While this would mitigate the incorrect transaction, it does hold Bitcoin users entirely responsible for these interactions. In any case, if careful

---

10 The New York Bar That Accepts Bitcoins. Fox, Emily Jane. CNN Money. © 2013 Cable News Network. A Time Warner Company. All Rights Reserved. http://money.cnn.com/2013/04/08/investing/bitcoin-bar-new-york-city/index.html

measures are taken to ensure the transaction is correct and the individual's wallet is secure when spending Bitcoins, this, and similar problems, can be avoided altogether.

When it comes to trading for Bitcoins themselves, these transactions are managed predominantly through exchanges. Exchanges set up Bitcoin users on their own platform and allow users to buy and sell Bitcoins for real world currency. These exchanges also act as a place to store Bitcoins. Now if setting up exchanges to help manage the flow of Bitcoins from hand to hand sounds contrary to the original premise of Bitcoins, that's because in theory it is. Many Bitcoin supporters feel that these exchanges are demeaning to the currency's design, but in practice, these exchanges do have their uses. When Bitcoin was new, having a wallet backed up on a home computer meant that an individual's holdings were safe. Today, users have taken to leaving their wallets' security in the hands of these exchanges who offer measures on par with those of banks to protect the currency. The other main advantage of these exchanges is that they add a measure of trust to transactions. They are a collective of individuals whose purpose is to expedite peoples' ability to transact. They help users quickly and easily buy and sell Bitcoins for any currency they choose on a platform they trust to work efficiently for them. Those who are opposed to the existence of these exchanges should note that these exchanges work to further empower their users by making buying and selling a much more reliable process. Because of this, it is highly recommended that those new to Bitcoins start to utilize the currency through these exchanges if only to make certain that all transactions are secure.[11]

---

11 Currency Exchange. Bitcoin Wiki. Retrieved May 7, 2013, from https://en.bitcoin.it/wiki/Currency_exchange

What are the Concerns with Bitcoins?

Considering so much of this book will be focused on touting the strengths of Bitcoin, it is only fair that its weaknesses are addressed as well. Many people fear this new digital currency and what it means for online payments. Thus, only by addressing and allaying those concerns will people come to terms with Bitcoin.

Perhaps the greatest issue that people have with Bitcoin is that it is not backed by any sort of formal governmental structure. People are used to their currencies being the currency of choice for an entire nation, a legal tender that represents value for an enormous group of people. Everyone in that nation has decided upon and endorsed the notion that the dollar, the Euro, etc. is the official mechanism for transferring wealth. In large part, people appreciate the way that currency systems operate today. After all, the dollar's government backing allows for a medium of exchange that is accepted throughout the United States. Though the dollar is subject to the monetary policies of those holding public office, currency can be trusted as an institution in its own right. The U.S Department of the Treasury maintains the value of the currency and prints more or less money depending on the current state of inflation. The reason this kind of backing is supported by people is that there's some entity that they can trust in. Bitcoin is backed by no one but its users, a network of individuals with holdings in the digital currency. The price of the currency will float up and down without any kind of guiding hand, and while the amount of Bitcoins is regulated by the system, the rate at which they are actually released is entirely up to the efforts of Bitcoin miners.[12]

Government backing also effectively guarantees that banks and other financial institutions must follow certain guidelines and act honestly and ethically. The penalty of the law remains a consequence for those who do not. In this way, these currencies maintain predictable, reliable systems that can be utilized to their full extent, which includes the financial well being of the average person. If some incredible wrong is done to an individual by a financial institution, the government will assure that individual's liberties are protected and justice will be done. With Bitcoins however, there is a complete lack of protection. When paying for anything with a credit card online, if there is any kind of issue, an individual can simply ask their credit card company or bank to dispute that charge on their behalf. This offers a layer of protection for every online transaction made. Bitcoin users have no such option. If there is some sort of difficulty with the transaction the individual must deal with it themselves by contacting whomever they transacted with. Even then, there is no guarantee that the issue will be dealt with fairly or at all. If nothing else, the United States

---

12 Bitcoin: Whatever it is, It's Not Money! Forbes, Steve. 2013 Forbes.com LLC™ All Rights Reserved. http://www.forbes.com/sites/steveforbes/2013/04/16/bitcoin-whatever-it-is-its-not-money/

has the FDIC to insure the money deposited in banks by its citizens. Aside from its other responsibilities, the FDIC will make sure that if a bank fails, those with holdings will receive the assets that the bank lost. Bitcoin lacks this measure of security that so many people are accustomed to and expect from a currency, and why so many people are nervous about Bitcoin's lack of formal structure.[13]

To many people, buying Bitcoins is like nailing a picture to a wall but not knowing if it will topple because there might not be anything holding up the other side. The concept of a digital currency that functions without a government behind it is confounding. In today's world that is full of uncertainties that fact is not comforting. The last few years alone have found turmoil in several major economies worldwide. In 2008, banks in the U.S. were found to be handing out mortgages like candy. This would lead to the collapse of the housing market that sent the nation into recession. In the same year, Bernie Madoff was arrested for an extensive Ponzi scheme that ruined the financial well being of a staggering number of people. With such rampant mistrust of banks, wealth management firms, and their ilk, it's no wonder why so many find themselves opposed to a currency based on cryptography. The idea is simply unfathomable. Why trust something that was created by a bunch of computer geeks when the institutions behind the dollar and where we put them have been so fragile?[13]

The fact of the matter is, for a fair number of people, the barriers to entry for Bitcoin are just too high. In order to attain a level of trust in the currency, there has to be a lot of explanation, something plain to see with this book. Bitcoin is not an easy

---

13 Federal Deposit Insurance Corporation. In Wikipedia. Retrieved May 8, 2013, from http://en.wikipedia.org/wiki/Federal_Deposit_Insurance_Corporation

sell. It requires knowledge of the way currencies work in the marketplace and an understanding of economics. Some people simply don't have the know-how or experience dealing with finances to trouble themselves with Bitcoin, while others don't have the technical expertise. Due to the electronic nature of the currency, many will not have been practiced at making purchases let alone purchasing currency online. The Bitcoin platform assumes that a majority of people not only have the technical savvy and economic understanding to navigate the websites of the currency's numerous proponents, but also have faith in their ability to utilize those skills and knowledge to safely acquire assets and invest wisely. The truth of it is that going from any paper currency to Bitcoin is a big step.

An issue that furthers the mistrust of Bitcoin is that the currency is entirely digital. There is no physical representation of it in the marketplace. At no bank can you withdraw Bitcoins like cash. This awakens an inherent discomfort with the currency. A common grievance is that Bitcoins are literally nothing but code inside of computers. The logical extension made from that statement is that it's extremely difficult to justify using a line of code as a representation of a store of value. There's no way to physically trade a line of code at the store to buy groceries, and many find that very off-putting. Much as it is easy to say that older generations take this issue in particular to heart, younger people have similar concerns. While the older crowd can say that Bitcoin changes an institution as old as society itself, younger generations see Bitcoins as another way in which people can point, click, and run their entire lives in front of a computer. An electronic currency seems a natural step. However, many younger people feel that Bitcoin serves to continue the expansion of the digital realm into reality in a way that seems unnecessary. Many younger people have used online payment methods for years now and have found that the dollar serves fine as a currency. From the perspective of those who do utilize the internet to make purchases, why change when things work? PayPal already exists in a form that makes online payments easy. Bitcoin is new and until such time that it proves its true worth, many may be unwilling to accept it as a viable currency.

The untraceable nature of Bitcoin transactions is yet another point of contention for those who oppose the currency's proliferation. The anonymity of Bitcoin has led to the rise of drug peddling sites such as the Silk Road where all manner of illicit substances were purchased. Though the site has since been shut down by the FBI, considering the amount of transactions involving these substances with Bitcoins, investing in the currency can prove to be a moral issue for many individuals. For those who are wholly against substance abuse, purchasing Bitcoins appears to be a blatant endorsement for such behavior to continue. The purchase and use of Bitcoins allows for the currency to continue to grow its user base and persevere in its efforts to be valued as a means for representing wealth. Without continued belief in the currency's value, it will cease to exist. In this way, using the currency while holding certain beliefs dear to heart proves to be a bit of a moral conundrum, one that Bitcoin itself cannot address. Assuredly, people will use money to buy what they wish regardless of legal consequences. However, the anonymity with which this can be done encourages this type of behavior and is frowned upon by many people.[14]

---

14 The Underground Website Where You Can Buy Any Drug Imaginable. Chen, Adrian. Gizmodo.com © Gawker Media 2013. http://gizmodo.com/5805928/

The other problem people have with the untraceable quality of Bitcoin transactions is that the lack of ability to track will harm their ability to personally dispute invalid transactions and follow through with legal action should there ever be an instance of theft. When using Bitcoins, as previously mentioned, every transaction is irreversible and as such, if a mistake were to be made in the payment process, it is up to the individual him/her-self to dispute the transaction. While the irreversible nature of these transactions could conceivably make this process difficult all on its own, the fact that its beneficiary is virtually untraceable proves a perilous obstacle to potential users. Imagine that an extra zero was tacked onto an online transaction by mistake to another individual for a good or service provided. While many Bitcoin users will freely provide their contact information in the event of some problem, many will not. This makes getting back those missing Bitcoins a nigh impossible prospect. The same could be said in a case of theft involving Bitcoins. While the stolen Bitcoins must be moved to a digital wallet on the network, though that wallet may be eventually be revealed, the criminal could simply use that throwaway wallet to transfer the Bitcoins anonymously to another untraceable digital wallet. It is through instances like these, which have actually happened, that people see Bitcoin as an opportunity for criminals to easily escape justice.[15]

Perhaps the greatest claim against Bitcoins is that regardless of its usefulness, no government accepts Bitcoins in lieu of its own currency to pay taxes. An individual may very well feel that Bitcoin is a great tool to conduct online purchases

---

the-underground-website-where-you-can-buy-any-drug-imaginable

15 Weaknesses. Bitcoin Wiki. Retrieved May 8, 2013, from https://en.bitcoin.it/wiki/Weaknesses

with and put all of his/her dollars into Bitcoins. However, if he/she still lives and works within the United States, he/she is subject to its tax laws. In this way, this individual's investiture in Bitcoins is really not worth much of anything. He/she can certainly pay for food and other such expenses in Bitcoins, but the fact is that the currency can't be used to pay his/her dues to the federal government. Therefore, unless you're planning to live on an island somewhere far away from society, Bitcoins will ultimately play the role of a secondary currency and fail to find widespread, regular usage.[16]

While it is true that if Bitcoins are devalued past the point of usability they will fail due to its lack of government backing, the same basic premise allows both the dollar and Bitcoin to survive. Any currency assumes that in order for a transaction to take place, all parties must agree on a medium of exchange that will be utilized in the transaction. In the case of the dollar, the government of the United States has deemed green printed paper and coins of a variety of different metals as its peoples' means of trading value. Collectively, the entire nation has agreed on this paper currency, and while once this paper was backed by gold, it is no longer backed by anything at all. Regardless of what value people ascribe to dollar bills, they are still green paper that provides no inherent purpose. Given that all paper currencies inherently provide no value in and of themselves, why can't Bitcoin act in the same exact manner? If we look at currency purely as a means to barter with other individuals, anything can be used as currency. The question everyone should ask themselves about using Bitcoins is why not? Societies making use of things other than paper and

16 Tax Compliance. Bitcoin Wiki. Retrieved May 8, 2013, from https://en.bitcoin.it/wiki/Tax_compliance

metal has been recorded numerous times throughout history. Seashells for instance, specifically cowry shells, were famously used in Africa as money.[17] With this in mind, are people at this point in history so enthralled by using paper and coins as a unit in monetary value that they refuse to give it up, or is it something more?[18]

It can be hypothesized that the true reason for the backlash against the practicality of using Bitcoins as a common currency stems from the fact that it is entirely digital. There is no physical representation of Bitcoins that can be held as paper money, as seashells, or as any other form of currency can be. That said, Bitcoins effectively do the exact same thing as dollars in the online payment space. While they cannot be used as cash for paying the kid who mows the lawn, they can enable your ability to purchase goods and services online much the same as the dollar can. There is an obvious hurdle to overcome in relying on a currency that is literally nothing more than code, but the same could be said of the money that is held in a bank. Banks can't possibly have an inventory of every dollar for every one of their clients' holdings. As a result, the money that individuals claim to have in their name is only a line of code in a computer system at the bank rather than their computer at home. The only difference between the two in that regard is that you cannot cash out your digital Bitcoins as physical Bitcoins.[18]

---

17 What were Seashells Used for in Ancient Times? Spirko, Jennifer. Ehow.com © 1999-2013 Demand Media, Inc. http://www.ehow.com/info_8676602_were-seashells-used-ancient-times.html

18 Digital Bitcoins Gain Prominence as Alternative to Fiat Currency. Newman, Alex. thenewamerican.com Copyright © 2012 Shaper Neo Demo. All Rights Reserved. http://www.thenewamerican.com/economy/economics/item/15128-digital-bitcoin-gains-prominence-as-alternative-to-fiat-currency

Many of Bitcoin's most avid supporters cite the lack of a government as a positive. Without monetary policies or any governmental department controlling the currency, Bitcoin is essentially free of human error and political agendas. No great, sweeping political changes will change the way Bitcoins works, nor effect how many are in existence at any given time. Bitcoin's functionality will remain fundamentally unchanged, whereas the dollar could be subject to any number of restrictions on the currency's use and circulation. While it is true that there is no federal body like the FDIC insuring Bitcoins if an exchange fails, many view this as a step towards empowering individuals with their finances. Ultimately, it is the individuals who are responsible for their Bitcoin transactions. Many feel that the nature of today's financial service companies lead people to believe that they no longer need to keep an eye on their money. History tells us something different, especially since 2008. Bitcoin passes all responsibility to the user, providing the individual with the power to do with their money as they will. Furthermore, the changes in Bitcoin's price are reflective of the market working effectively, not some problem with the currency. Given the limited number of Bitcoins, they will be valued at different prices as time goes on and as economic circumstances change. Though it may be strange to get used to and can be difficult to keep track of, this quirk is ultimately an advantage of the currency.

Bitcoin does make certain assumptions about those who wish to use the currency. Only those with experience regularly making online transactions and exchanging currency will truly feel at ease with the process of buying Bitcoins. However, it is for this very purpose that this book exists. The barriers to entry for Bitcoin involve the technical expertise needed to work with the currency. The fears that arise from these issues can only be dispelled through education. Veritable interest in Bitcoin will lead to a massive amount of books and articles with which anyone can be educated. With resources like this book and other guides and how-to manuals, jumping into the Bitcoin network should become a much less daunting prospect. Obviously for those who are inexperienced or dislike using the internet to buy and sell goods or services, Bitcoin is probably not for you. That said, as more and more services move to online spaces, Bitcoin may be something to look into.

The purchase of drugs and other illegal substances using Bitcoins has been a massive turn-off for many potential users. Those who are opposed to substance abuse don't want to own Bitcoins because they believe that the currency contributes to a group of drug peddlers and thieves. While usage of the currency does help such activities survive, ceasing Bitcoin's utilization won't prevent people from buying and selling illicit substances. If Bitcoin were to collapse as a currency, those people who were buying drugs with the digital currency would simply switch back to whatever currency they were using prior to Bitcoins. While Bitcoin does make it easier to buy and sell drugs, cash enables this behavior in the same way. With this in mind, it becomes plain to see that the mistrust in the Bitcoins does not arise from its users buying drugs; rather it comes from the ability of those with poor intentions and poorer ethics to utilize a certain feature of the currency to enable the existence of sites like the Silk Road. The fault lies not with either of these currencies but with the capacity for people to use them for purely legitimate purchases.[19]

---

19 This Illegal Drug Website is Taking Bitcoins for Tim Tams. Collins, Ben. au.businessInsider.com © 2007-2013 Allure Media. http://au.businessinsider.com/this-illegal-drugs-website-is-taking-bitcoins-for-tim-tams-2013-4

The feature that allows this kind of behavior is the anonymity of Bitcoin's transactions. Unfortunately, drug peddling isn't the only abuse that this feature experiences. However, those opposed to using Bitcoin who are weary of their ability to dispute claims personally should not fret overmuch. Though transactions are anonymous, they are only as anonymous as users make them. Whenever Bitcoins are transferred, a user sends the currency via a Bitcoin address. The user who receives the currency can see that address and track it to its owner. Though an individual may have as many addresses as desired, many people, regardless of how many addresses they have, will be candid and forthcoming with contact information in the event of a problem. The thing to remember about Bitcoin is that it allows for users to rely on themselves for the safety of their holdings.

The digital nature of the currency is a pain point that Bitcoin cannot provide any real rebuke to. No, there is no physical representation of the currency. However, it should be noted that its lack of physicality does provide some benefits. One is that Bitcoin's entirely digital existence saves more trees than its paper counterparts. Another boon is that it can be very easily accounted for with regards to taxes. While it does remain a problem that taxes themselves cannot be paid for in Bitcoins, the proper accounting for transactions utilizing the currency is possible and easily accessible. Lastly, the lack of a physical presence means that Bitcoins cannot be stolen as a credit card could be and renders identity theft nearly impossible. Bitcoin wallets don't need to have any personal information attached to them and thus, none of that information could be lost in the event of some kind of hacking attempt.

Are Bitcoins Similar to Gold and Silver?

Bitcoin has been consistently compared to gold and silver throughout its existence, and for good reason. Bitcoins, like gold and silver, are stores of value and objects of speculation that serve the economic system in just this way.[20] While gold and silver do have some practical purposes, they are largely viewed as commodities, or simple objects of value. It was for this reason that the U.S. dollar was once backed by gold and silver. Essentially, every dollar printed represented the amount of gold that could be exchanged for that dollar. Because of the gold's inherent value, the money representing it held value as its legal tender. Eventually the U.S. government realized that this policy was not sustainable as there were limited ways to print more currency without devaluing the dollar considerably. Thus, since 1971, the ideal of having a gold standard for printed currency has been abandoned.[21]

---

20 Why the Price of Gold is Plummeting: Six Theories. Cassidy, John. © 2013 Condé Nast. All rights reserved. http://www.newyorker.com/online/blogs/johncassidy/2013/04/gold-price-bitcoin-goldman-china-inflation.html

21 Pros and Cons of the Gold Standard. Energybackedmoney.com © 2009 EnergyBackedMoney.com Published: 11/2009 Last Updated: 1/2012. http://www.energybackedmoney.com/chapter4.html

If Bitcoin's foundation bears more than a passing resemblance to the gold standard, there is good reason: the platform was designed with just this type of valuation in mind. Obviously the biggest difference is the fact that Bitcoins are not backed by anything except Bitcoins, but otherwise, the similarities are striking. In both cases the idea is that the object's limited supply gives it value. Dollars represent the amount of value of gold that is placed on a good. Bitcoins represent the digital value that is placed on that same good. In today's economy where the gold standard is no longer applicable, both dollars and Bitcoins are valued simply because they are a means to an end. They allow their users to transfer value from their own coffers into another's. However, where Bitcoin deviates from other currencies is in its ability to remain limited. More dollars can be printed at any time to deflate its value. Bitcoins cannot be artificially reproduced to achieve some political objective or mitigate fluctuating prices. It must be created and introduced to its community who knows that only so many new Bitcoins can ever be revealed.

The similarities don't stop at this cursory glance. Even the way new Bitcoins are obtained takes its ideas from gold as a standard for currency. Much as mining for gold is a means to attempt to introduce more of a commodity of value into the economic system, mining for Bitcoins is an attempt to introduce entirely new currency to the Bitcoin network. Bitcoin mining was specifically modeled after the California Gold Rush of 1848. At the beginning of the gold rush, miners had but to sift through the dirt and sand from the riverbeds to discover flecks of gold, but sifting quickly turned to pickaxes, and soon after that only heavy machinery could find the precious metal. Over time, both the difficulty of obtaining gold and the barriers to entry for mining increased exponentially. The same can be said of the process of mining Bitcoins. At its introduction, mining for Bitcoins could be done with a single ordinary computer. Now that 13 million or so Bitcoins have already been found, it is both difficult to unearth one and expensive to do so considering both material and energy costs.

Perhaps the most striking similarity between gold, silver, and Bitcoins is that there is a limited supply of all of them. Only so many bars of gold and silver, and real Bitcoins can ever be available to the economy at any given time. While Bitcoins have no physical presence, their value is derived from the same desire to obtain them that people have to obtain gold and silver. This is why the prices of all of these things are speculated on to such a great extent. There is demand for them. In the case of gold, there is a demand for the shiny metal that can be traded for other objects of value. For Bitcoins, the demand stems from the desire of many people to utilize a protocol for a separate international currency. Either way, this leads to the valuation of gold and Bitcoins, respectively, which leads to the speculation of the prices of both of these commodities.

It has been said that Bitcoins share the benefits of gold but lack its downsides. One example is that if gold functioned as a standard for currency today, its real world ability to have a limited supply would serve to add value to the metal. However, if there was suddenly an incredible increase in the amount of gold available it would wildly reduce the purchasing power of the money backed by it. Bitcoin does not have this problem. There are a set amount of Bitcoins in existence and there cannot be more Bitcoins created than are already in the system, which is a fact known by all of its users. Mining does not actually create new Bitcoins, it simply reveals their existence to the network. As a result, their addition does not devalue the currency, but rather incentivizes users to attempt to obtain more Bitcoins before they are all mined or the mining difficulty becomes too great.[22]

Another example is the inefficiency of mining gold as compared to Bitcoins. Mining gold requires a massive amount of overhead to obtain any meaningful amount. It is estimated that in 2014 the average cost for mining gold would be $1,200 per ounce.[23] Extrapolating that cost out to a much larger scale equates to a massive expenditure for a metal that will be plucked from the earth, reshaped, and more often than not, shoved into a vault. If this seems like a massive exhaustion of resources, that's because it is. Bitcoins, on the other hand, are mined using computers. The only resource used up is electricity. While it is far from a cheap endeavor to mine Bitcoins at this point, the cost of power to mine for a year on the average laptop is roughly $200. The entire mining costs for a day are about $147,000 in the US. That $147,000 in electricity recently yielded roughly $681,000 in profit.[24] While it can be argued that the amount of energy being utilized for mining Bitcoins is electricity that could have been used to provide power to homes across the country, that amount is paltry when put into perspective. Bitcoin mining accounts for about .025% of the electricity costs for the nation's 120 million people.

22 Why Bitcoins are Just like Gold. Liu, Alice. © 2013 Vice Media Inc.http://motherboard.vice.com/blog/why-bitcoins-are-just-like-gold

23 Stepping into Gold Miners' Shoes. Seekingalpha.com © 2013 Seeking Alpha.http://seekingalpha.com/article/1345781-stepping-in-gold-miners-shoes?-source=google_news

24 Bitcoin Miners Generating High Electricity Bills. BBC.co.uk BBC © 2013. http://www.bbc.co.uk/news/technology-22153687

Though this is still a respectable portion of electricity that could be utilized elsewhere, it is important to recognize that at some point in the future the electricity expenses incurred from Bitcoin mining will slow and eventually decline drastically. Due to the ever increasing difficulty curve of mining and the currency's limited supply, mining will eventually become too arduous or there simply won't be any Bitcoins left to mine. Because of this, these electricity costs will be eradicated or too negligible to mention. All that will be left are the energy costs incurred by the processing of transactions, which are costs that exist with any sort of online payment system. In these terms, Bitcoins are a much more efficient currency to produce, and further proves Bitcoin's lack of similarity to gold with regard to its more negative aspects.[25]

Will Bitcoins Survive?

Many may think that Bitcoin will come and go due to its similarities with other currencies or currency standards like gold and silver. There are, however, some major differences that lend to the belief that Bitcoin will survive its current stature as a novelty currency and become a viable and popular method of payment.

As an emerging technology, Bitcoin's rises and falls have been likened to the Hype Cycle. In a hype cycle, the first thing that occurs is that a technology such as Bitcoin emerges. In this case, Bitcoin was invented and implemented and has found early success. Next, expectations rise dramatically, usually in unrealistic proportion to what the technology

25 Bitcoin Mining is Not a Real World Financial Disaster. Worstall, Tim. 2013 Forbes.com LLC™ All Rights Reserved. http://www.forbes.com/sites/tim-worstall/2013/04/14/bitcoin-mining-is-not-a-real-world-environmental-disaster/

actually offers. At this stage, there are people throwing their hopes at the technology finding both success and failure with the new medium on a much larger scale. Following that is a general disillusionment with the technology. Either the technology has become stale or does not offer what it promises, and the rate of adoption drops. Should the technology survive its inevitable decline in interest, it will experience a revival as the merits and benefits of the technology become better understood. Finally, the technology becomes widely adopted and accepted, its relevance fully comprehended.[26]

Currently, there seems to be steady growing interest in Bitcoin as a means to regularly conduct online business. As the second graph below suggests, Bitcoin is well on its way to becoming a legitimate, widely used technology. However, it is difficult to truly place Bitcoin exactly on a hype cycle. It has experienced a great deal of volatility throughout its existence and while many love the concept and the platform's functionality, many are not sold on its benefits as a separate currency. In any event, it seems fair to say that Bitcoin's upward mobility is trending and given time it may reach the point of widespread acceptance as more people see its advantages.[27]

---

26 Hype Cycles. Gartner.com © 2013 Gartner, Inc. and/or its Affiliates. All Rights Reserved. http://www.gartner.com/technology/research/methodologies/hype-cycle.jsp

27 Bitcoin Breaks All Time High. Buterin, Vitalik. bitcoinmagazine.com © Copyright 2013 © Coin Publishing Ltd. http://bitcoinmagazine.com/bitcoin-price-breaks-all-time-high/

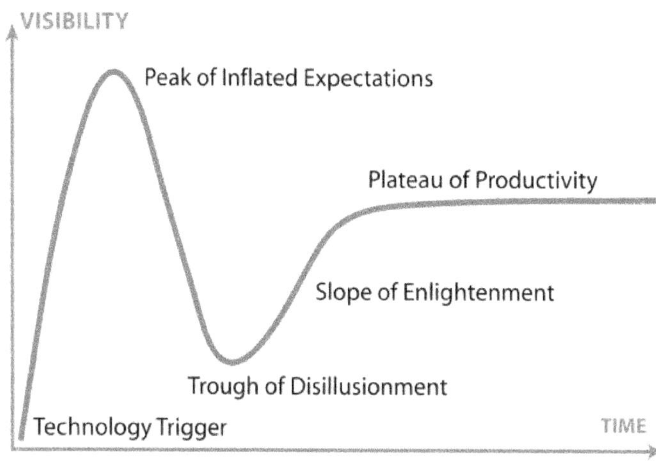

Figure 1: Graph of a simple hype cycle.

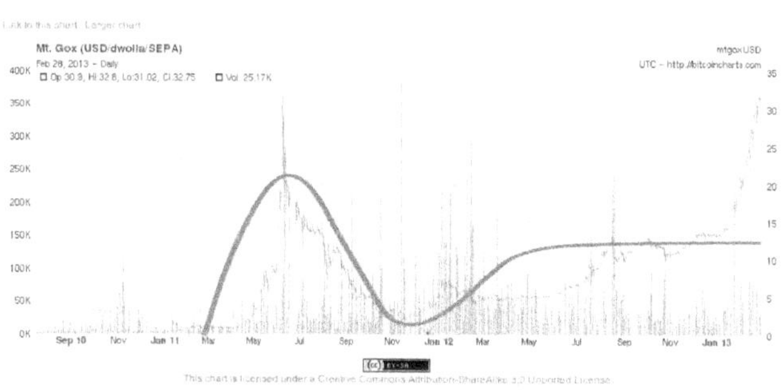

Figure 2: Graph of a hype cycle superimposed over Bitcoin's life cycle.

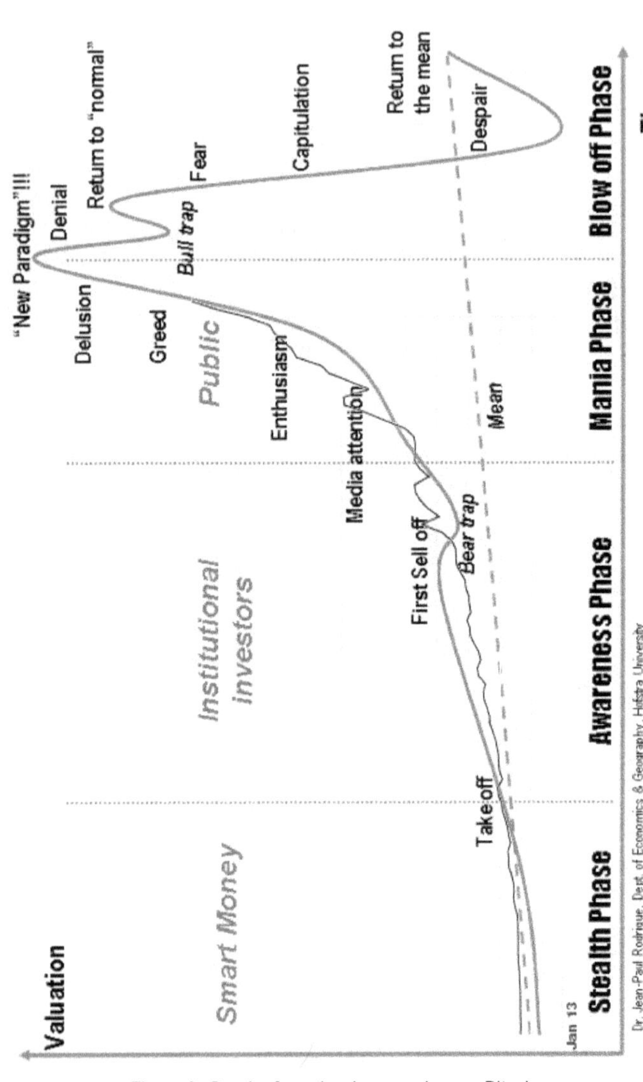

Figure 3: Graph of another hype cycle over Bitcoin, predicting the future life cycle of the currency.[28]

---

28 Bitcoin – Believe the Hype. Retrieved May 8, 2013, from wallstreetoasis.com © 2006-2012 WallStreetOasis.com | All Rights Reserved. http://www.wallstreetoasis.com/blog/bitcoin-believe-the-hype

A remarkable feature of Bitcoin is that it has no central authority and is not backed by any government. This, as you may have seen, is why there can be incredible fluxes in price and demand, as that aspect of the currency is solely dictated by its users. This can potentially be very off putting and understandably so. After all, it can become tiresome to attempt to keep track of the going rate of the currency you're paying in when there are large differences in its value from one day to the next. However, upon closer inspection, this setup may be perfect. Basic economic principles tell us that when supply diminishes, demand, and further, price rises and vice versa. Because currency in and of itself has only perceived value, it can artificially inflate due to the perceived capabilities that it provides to its users. The price of Bitcoins has, and will, inflate based on its worth as a placeholder for value for this reason. The value of a Bitcoin can vary considerably given other economic factors as well. Bitcoins recently experienced an incredible increase in price due to the financial crisis in Cyprus. Many used Bitcoin as a way to secure their financial position and hedge themselves against bank account seizures. Soon afterwards, the artificially raised price of Bitcoin dropped significantly back down to reflect its actual value to users.[29]

It is important to note that the term users was utilized here and not some authoritative figure. In the end, the users of the currency drive the price of Bitcoin. The point to consider here is that because Bitcoin has no institution regulating price, the currency acts as a perfect example of a simple, enclosed economic system in which the only good is the

---

29 Bitcoin. Bitcoin Wiki. Retrieved May 8, 2013, from https://en.bitcoin.it/wiki/Bitcoin

Bitcoin. Bitcoins are completely free of human error, politics, and monetary policies of other national currencies. The price of the currency reacts according to speculation and realization of actual economic events. In this way, Bitcoin acts as a pure currency and lends credence to its survivability. If its users retain confidence in Bitcoin's ability to remain a viable currency for exchange, which in theory it should be and thus far in practice it has been, then it will not only continue to be used but its user base will grow significantly. As Bitcoin usage grows, it will become more and more accepted throughout the world and will find its survival not easily threatened.[30]

The success of Bitcoin is due in no small part to the animosity that people have developed for banks and other financial institutions. The last five years have seen multiple financial crises throughout the world. Even the largest nations have felt the effects of some financial disaster or another, and Bitcoin itself may have been created in reaction to the mortgage crisis of 2008 in the United States. With this in mind, it is no wonder that so many see Bitcoin as a refreshing look at life without big banks and politically driven monetary policies. There is no central bank that can print more Bitcoins. No authority setting a price level for the currency. Bitcoins are currency in a form that empowers people. Bitcoins have no physical presence and no ascribed practical value. Bitcoins are whatever its users will them to be. The value placed on Bitcoins is the value that users subjectively place on them.

What's more is that the Bitcoin is a network that sustains itself because people have a desire for the functionality of the currency. Bitcoin is not currently part of the world economy because it was willed into existence by any government; it

30 FAQ. Bitcoin Wiki. Retrieved May 8, 2013, from https://en.bitcoin.it/wiki/FAQ

survives because people feel that there is value in the currency and what the platform can achieve. Regardless of the present value of a Bitcoin, the mean value of the currency will continue to increase because people are becoming increasingly aware of its utility. As more people use the currency, more people will contribute to the network, and in essence, ensure its continued prosperity.

The gradual release of Bitcoins into its economy has spurred this very occurrence. As Bitcoin generation slows, the currency rises in value because of the realization of its scarcity. Bitcoin mining was designed in such a way that the currency's release into the market would be tempered as interest for the currency increased. This functions as a way to maintain that there are never too many Bitcoins for the amount of demand in the marketplace, nor too few. This is done by increasing the difficulty of mining as more Bitcoins are obtained. In other words, as more people want to acquire Bitcoins and actively mine them, less and less are actually obtained. This increases the desirability of the currency and raises its value to users. Without this feature in place, Bitcoins would either be released too quickly into the economy or too slowly. In both scenarios, interest for Bitcoins would stagnate completely. There would either be so many Bitcoins that their value would depreciate past the point of anyone caring or there would be too few for anyone to obtain and the currency would find itself limited in value before its uses diminished entirely. Either way, these occurrences would kill the currency.

However, with this feature automating the release of funds accordingly, demand for Bitcoins should remain intact. The currency is created to allow for the existence of inverse relationships between the number of people actively mining and obtaining Bitcoins and the amount and difficulty of actually acquiring the currency. Thus, as the amount of people mining and using Bitcoin as a currency increases, its value will increase right along with it. This serves to both incite people to take interest in the currency, and increase the demand and the value of the Bitcoin over time.

All things considered, it appears as though Bitcoin is here to stay. With numerous measures in place to ensure the currency's survival, it seems unlikely that it will disappear any time soon. People find value in what Bitcoin offers. If nothing else, people believe that the currency should theoretically function very well in today's globally connected society. Many recognize the need for an electronic currency given the amount of online transactions there are daily. It seems that as time goes on, digital currency will likely find itself more ingrained in the everyday lives of the people of the information age, which is a prospect that makes Bitcoin ever more promising.[31]

What are the Facts and Fiction about Bitcoins?

The following are some facts and statistics that will serve to better your understanding of Bitcoin. They are juxtaposed alongside so-called myths about the currency. These commonly held beliefs are markedly untrue, as explained below:

Myths:

- *Bitcoins are predominantly used for buying/selling drugs.*

---

31 Bitcoin Outshine's Canada's Stalled Mintchip. George-Cosh, David. Wsj.com Copyright ©2013 Dow Jones & Company, Inc. All Rights Reserved. http://blogs.wsj.com/canadarealtime/2013/04/19/bitcoin-outshines-canadas-stalled-mintchip/

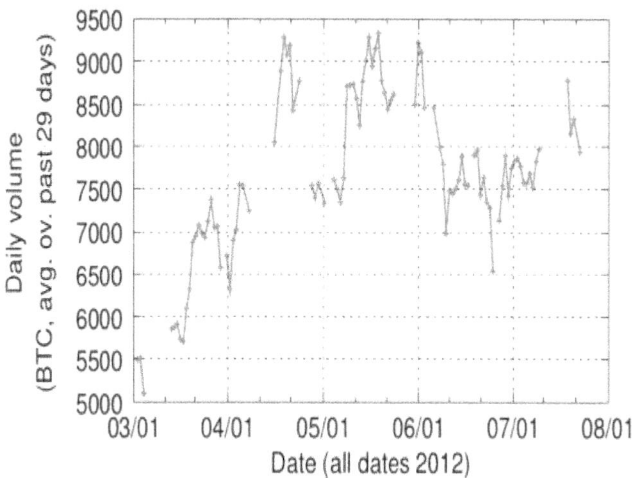

Figure 4: Graph of the total daily sales that occurred on the Silk Road, used to illustrate volume.[32] Each point corresponds to an average over the prior 29 days.

Understandably one of the greatest concerns with Bitcoin is that it fuels black market items like illegal drugs and weapons. The nature of Bitcoin allows for transactions to remain anonymous. Because of this suppliers of illegal items have flocked to Bitcoin as a means to peddle their wares without fear of incurring the wrath of the law. This should in no way dissuade honest, law abiding citizens from using Bitcoin. Cash is used every day to make anonymous purchases of illicit goods yet people still use the dollar. The short of it is that Bitcoin should not be judged based on the choices that some of its users make when so many others are utilizing the currency to make entirely ordinary online purchases. The above graph would have you believe that most every Bitcoin is spent on drugs. Funnily enough, some of the most popular purchases on the well-known, though now defunct drug vending site The

32 Silk Road: Theory and Practice. Created: 27 Jan 2009 modified: 07 May 2013. Retrieved May 8, 2013, from http://www.gwern.net/Silk%20Road

Silk Road were snacks from other countries. In summation, while some people wielding Bitcoins are dastards after mind altering drugs, some people are just in it for the sweets.

➢ *Bitcoin is no different from other currencies because more Bitcoins can always be created.*

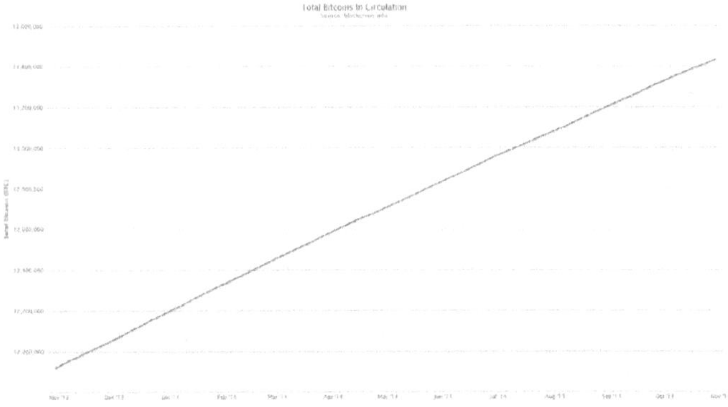

Figure 5: Graph of the total number of Bitcoins in circulation. The increase is gradual and predictable.[33]

There are a finite number of Bitcoins that will ever be in existence. The graph above shows the number of Bitcoins currently available in the market. Over time, the number of Bitcoins that are available increases, but as more are made available, they become more difficult to obtain. This serves to increase the value of the currency as time goes on as interest in using Bitcoin rises. This feature makes Bitcoin different than other currencies because typically, as time wares on, the currency becomes devalued. Bitcoin does not have this issue because unlike other currencies, Bitcoins cannot be reproduced or copied. More are revealed to the network but

---

33 Total Bitcoins in Circulation. Reeves, Ben. Blockchain.info. http://blockchain.info/charts/total-bitcoins

no new Bitcoins are ever made, thus retaining and increasing the currency's value instead of reducing it.

- *Mining for Bitcoins is no longer profitable. The mining difficulty has increased to the point that the cost of the electricity to mine Bitcoins far outweighs potential gains.*

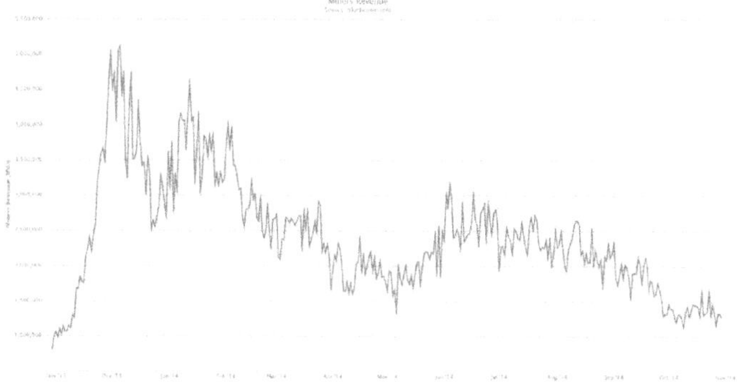

Figure 6: Graph depicting the revenue of miners over a year's time. Revenue is fairly consistent.[34]

Mining for Bitcoins has remained a profitable venture even as the mining difficulty increases. It may not be profitable to mine Bitcoins individually as it once was, but collectively the venture can still be lucrative as the graph above shows. Recently there has been an arms race with regards to mining technology to see who could turn out the most powerful processor for the sole purpose of Bitcoin mining. While hardware for effective Bitcoin mining has become more and more expensive, pools have formed to help lower the barriers to entry for those interested in earning more of the

34 Miners Revenue. Reeves, Ben. Blockchain.info. http://blockchain.info/charts/miners-revenue

currency. These pools facilitate cooperation between groups of machines in order to more effectively mine for Bitcoins. Any Bitcoins earned by the pool are disseminated amongst its contributors according to their input.

Ultimately, this graph proves that the notion of the inefficiency of Bitcoin mining is false, as the process still turns a profit. It is also an excellent example of the way Bitcoin was designed to continue to thrive as more and more people utilize the currency.

➢ *Merchants don't accept Bitcoins as payments and consumers don't use the currency to purchase things online. People just hoard Bitcoins.*

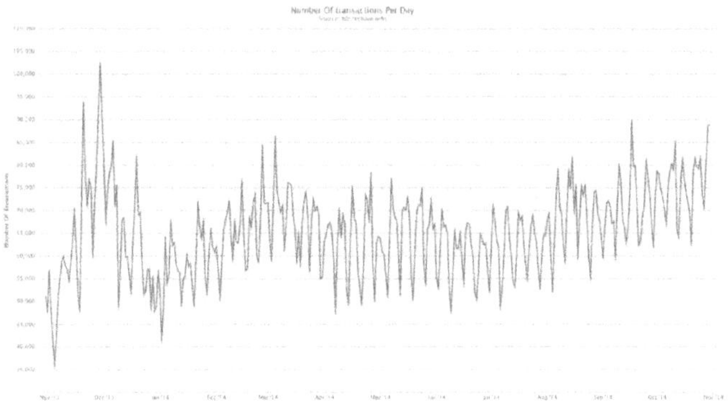

Figure 7: Graph depicting the growing number of transactions per day in Bitcoins.[35]

While it is true that Bitcoins aren't as widely accepted as other currencies as payment, the popularity of Bitcoin usage is definitely on the rise. The graph above illustrates the increase in the number of transactions per day using Bitcoins.

35 Number of Transactions Per Day. Reeves, Ben. Blockchain.info. http://blockchain.info/charts/n-transactions

The growth of usage for the currency appears to have picked up speed of late and is steadily rising. If nothing else, the data indicates that the amount of people utilizing the currency is on the rise. If more people try Bitcoins and find it to be an acceptable alternative to other currencies, it will continue to thrive in economies throughout the world. It may have been once that Bitcoins were just hoarded, but as time goes on, those hoarders are finding uses for their stashed currency as more vendors accept Bitcoins.

- *This currency is a fad that is only appealing overseas. No one in the Americas is taking Bitcoin seriously.*

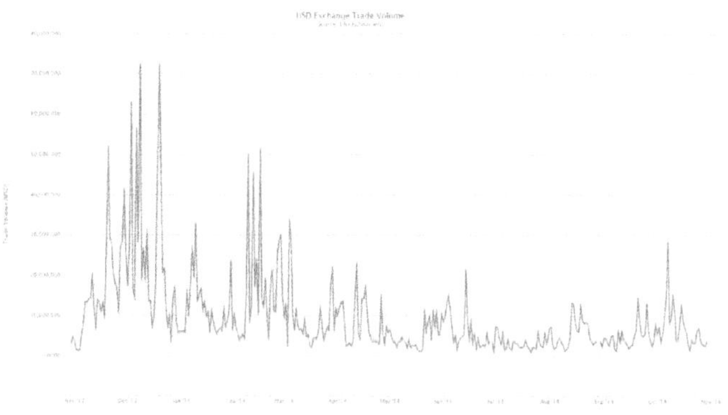

Figure 8: Graph of the USD exchange trade volume in Bitcoins over a year's time.[36]

36 USD Exchange Trade Volume. Reeves, Ben. Blockchain.info. http://blockchain.info/charts/trade-volume

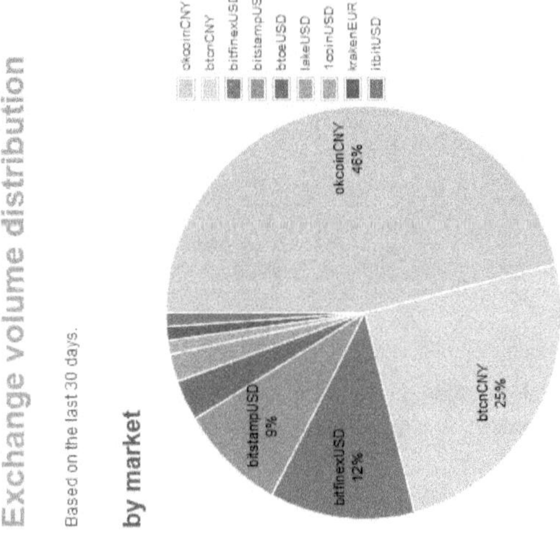

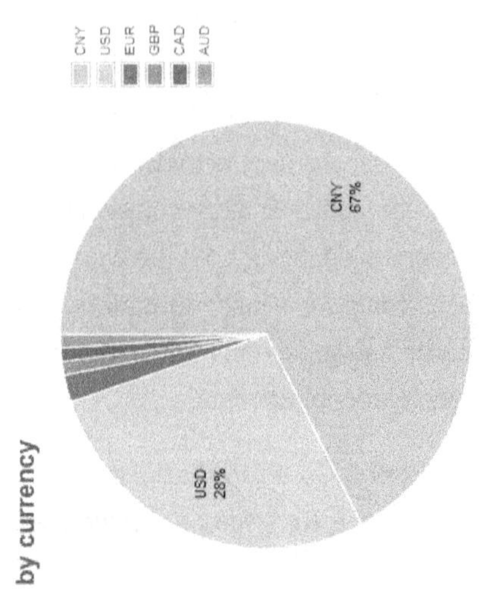

Figure 9: Pie charts of Bitcoin's exchange volume distribution by market and by currency.[37]

37 Exchange Volume Distribution. © bitcoincharts.com. http://bitcoincharts.com/charts/volumepie/

This statement has become less and less true over time. As the first graph shows, Bitcoin exchanges involving the U.S. dollar have remained relatively consistent over time. This is reflective of the incredible amount of interest Bitcoin has garnered in the United States. If the second graph is any indication of things to come, it seems more and more apparent that Bitcoin will find people willing to adopt the currency all over the world. While the largest amount of transactions currently involves the US dollar, the Chinese Yuan, and the Euro, many other national currencies are represented, further supporting the claim that Bitcoin usage is making its way around the world. Additionally, that 28% of Bitcoin exchanges occur in USD goes to show the amount of serious interest there is in the digital currency.

- *Bitcoin transactions are not as quick and convenient as other methods of online payment, chiefly credit cards.*

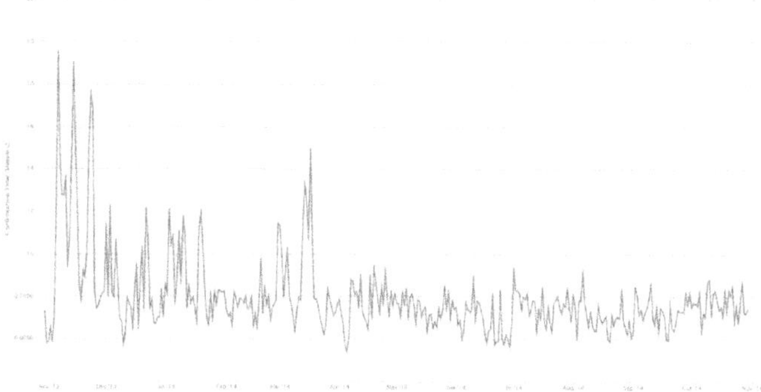

Figure 10: Graph of the average transaction confirmation time, which is gradually dwindling.[38]

38 Average Transaction Confirmation Time. Reeves, Ben. Blockchain.info. http://blockchain.info/charts/avg-confirmation-time

As shown above, the time it takes for the network to confirm each transaction is short and has remained largely consistent over time. Through the process of mining, Bitcoin can provide fast transactions without the fees that are typically incurred using other currencies. This is something Bitcoin's supporters tout as yet another reason why the currency will remain relevant and grow into a serious competitor with regards to buying and selling online.

➢ *Other interesting Bitcoin facts:*

- The first known real-world Bitcoin transaction was made in 2010 in Florida when two pizzas was purchased and delivered from Papa John's for 10,000 Bitcoins. As of a few weeks ago, those Bitcoins the pizzas were paid with would have been worth a little over $2 million.[39]
- In 2010 police mistakenly raided a man's home due to his Bitcoin mining. His electricity bill was so high that the police believed he was growing marijuana inside of his house.[40]
- You can buy alpaca socks with Bitcoins: http://www.grasshillalpacas.com/alpacaproductsforbitcoinoffer.html

---

39 Meet the $2 Million Bitcoin Pizza. Hit and Run Blog. ©2012 Reason Foundation. Mangu-Ward, Katherine. http://reason.com/blog/2013/04/09/meet-the-2-million-bitcoin-pizza

40 Bitcoin Miners Busted? Police Confuse Bitcoin Power Usage for Pot Farm. Storm, Darlene. Computerworld.com. Copyright © 1994 - 2013 Computerworld Inc. All rights reserved. http://blogs.computerworld.com/18335/bitcoin_miners_busted_police_confuse_bitcoin_power_usage_for_pot_farm

- This guy wrote a song about Bitcoin, and it's actually not terrible: http://www.youtube.com/watch?v=pYqq-S7aTBVQ&feature=player_embedded
- A woman actually lived off Bitcoins successfully for a week: http://www.forbes.com/sites/kash-mirhill/2013/05/01/living-on-bitcoin-for-a-week-the-journey-begins/

How Can I Make Money with Bitcoin?

Now that we have an understanding of what Bitcoin is, how it works, and why it's a winner, a big question remains: how can someone make money with Bitcoin? The first thing that any savvy investor should do is get into the game. If Bitcoin is going to be profitable, regardless of how long it has already been out there, getting involved is the only way to profit along with it.

Before we go into detail as to how it's possible to make money with Bitcoin, it's of extreme importance to remember that at its core, Bitcoins are currency. Bitcoins are intended to be utilized for online transactions as a medium for delivering value from one person to the next for whatever good or service is offered. Bitcoin is not innately some money making scheme. It was created to allow like-minded individuals to take a step back from banks and politics and the fiscal policies of governments and put power back into the hands of individuals. The currency should be respected for what it is and what it is trying to do. Once this is understood, we can move forward and work within the platform to profit.

One potentially profitable venture involving Bitcoins is mining for the currency. While Bitcoin mining is profitable for those who are committed to the process, it is well past the point where an individual can make any substantial profit by mining alone without incurring incredible expenses. Solving a block amounts to about $1,000 worth of electricity and will cost at least $1,000 in hardware. If a computer was to be built for the sole purpose of mining, the hardware needed to efficiently work out the blockchain's mathematical problems would cost several thousands of dollars and cost nearly as much in electricity every day. Because of this, numerous mining pools have been formed to merge the processing power of many like minded Bitcoin users to mine cooperatively. By utilizing pools mining has been very profitable. The benefits of mining with a pool are that that it both increases the odds of actually finding Bitcoins and keeps the cost of finding them far lower than they would be otherwise. Statistically, given that only so many people will complete the algorithms to produce Bitcoins, and considering that the difficulty of solving these algorithms has increased significantly since Bitcoin's introduction, it is in a miner's best interest to join a pool.

Bitcoin mining is a fairly simple process that requires only a minor amount of preparation prior to its commencement. The first step is to obtain a wallet for your Bitcoins. There is no shortage of wallet providers to choose from so my best advice is to use a provider who appears trustworthy and stable; blockchain.info is popular for one but a wallet from many other providers will prove to be just as suitable, including wallets provided by exchanges like Bitstamp. The next step is to download Bitcoin mining software; bitcoinx.com has a list of different programs that allow you to mine Bitcoins. Typically these programs will walk you through how to use them and are free to download. Many programs offer the ability to directly contribute to specific mining pools so that you can share in the profits of any blocks created. With a powerful enough system, Bitcoin mining can be profitable. While it may have a disheartening price tag of $6,800, the Avalon ASIC is currently the best computing system for mining. Currently, it is capable of producing roughly four Bitcoins per day, which can be exchanged for a considerable amount of money. This, however, is only suggested for individuals with deep pockets who are wholly committed to Bitcoin mining.[41]

If mining seems like a daunting challenge a great alternative is to purchase a mining contract. Rather than purchasing an expensive Bitcoin mining unit and covering the high electricity costs, the folks at cloudhashing.com offer up their own computing power to mine for you. They have recognized that there is serious interest in Bitcoins and the mining process but many people lack the resources, the technical knowledge, or the time to do it. Thus, they are selling their processing power by the Gigahashes, or computing power, to mine Bitcoins. With a single purchase, a Bitcoin user can receive a steady flow of the currency every two weeks based upon the size of the contract he/she bought. You may have to pay for your contract in Bitcoins but if the currency's user base continues to grow, that investment may pay off quite nicely, especially considering the lack of personal involvement. As long as an individual can pay for the contract, he/she does not need to actively

41 Want to make money off Bitcoin mining? Hint: Don't mine. Gayomali, Chris. Theweek.com © 2013 the Week Publications, Inc. All Rights Reserved. http://theweek.com/article/index/242753/want-to-make-money-off-bitcoin-mining-hint-dont-mine

mine Bitcoins and will get the currency they earned with their contract regularly with no hassle. It's a pretty ingenious solution that doesn't require a massive investment and gets people involved with Bitcoins. Obviously the biggest concern with this type of investment is that the provider of the opportunity must be trustworthy, else they'll simply take your non-refundable Bitcoin investment and run. Because of this, again, it is wise only to use providers you deem reliable and legitimate.[42]

Another opportunity to profit with Bitcoin is to utilize its ability to make foreign exchange transactions in favor of the currency you are using. Bitcoin can be viewed as a currency exchange market where people are constantly using dollars to buy Bitcoins, and get Bitcoins with Yen and use Yen to buy more Bitcoins and so on. Currencies are changing hands rapidly at Bitcoin exchanges. Anyone on these exchanges watching the prices of these currencies can take advantage of the differences in the values attached to them. It can hypothetically be cheaper to buy Bitcoins with Euros than dollars. Thus, if a user had Euros, they could buy Bitcoins with that currency and then exchange those Bitcoins on the network for a higher price in dollars. This requires paying a good deal of attention to many different currencies with respect to Bitcoin but it can certainly be done and become a profitable venture. There are many websites that allow you to do just this sort of trading like icbit.se and bitfinex.com for instance. As always, please be careful with whom you are dealing with while buying and selling Bitcoins. If you exhibit caution with trades it will keep your funds safe.[43]

---

42 How Does it All Work. Cloudhashing.com All Rights Reserved. © 2013 | CloudHashing.com. https://www.cloudhashing.com/how-we-work

43 Currency Exchange. Bitcoin Wiki. Retrieved May 8, 2013, from Currency Exchange. https://en.bitcoin.it/wiki/Currency_exchange

If after reading all of the reasons why Bitcoin will survive and you don't believe in the probability of future success for the digital currency, there are opportunities to make money as a result of its failure, or at least there will be. Coinsetter.com claims that by using their Bitcoin trading platform they will "allow you to leverage your trades and short the market with [their] professional, transparent platform". Kraken.com claims it will be offering similar services as well. Keep in mind that this opportunity does require a firm grasp of investment knowledge, chiefly how to pair currencies and leverage them accordingly. Similar opportunities exist by way of dwolla.com and btcjam.com wherein an individual is able to take out loans in dollars for Bitcoins, and then lend those Bitcoins out at a higher interest rate than the original loan. If the Bitcoin falls in price, the individual to whom you loaned Bitcoins would owe you more than what you gave them. Then, upon paying back the original loan, there would theoretically be a net profit in dollars because of the differing interest rates. A note of import is that this is a risky investment.[44] Bitcoin is known to be highly volatile of late and an investment of this sort falls within a desperately unregulated area. Because of this, the best suggestion for this type of financial endeavor would be to invest at your own risk and to not stake too much on these speculations. Though the current state of investing against Bitcoin is uncertain and challenging, the growing interest in the currency will soon give way to a rise demand for more promising opportunities to short sell. The addition of short selling opportunities will most notably serve to more efficiently manage the liquidity of the currency by providing a veritable smorgasbord of eager buyers and sellers. As a result, Bitcoin

---

44 A Peer to Peer Bitcoin Lending Network. Cardoso, Celso. Btcjam.com Copyright © 2012 Ovo Cósmico LTDA. https://btcjam.com/how_it_works/overview

usage will grow. More people will utilize the currency and draw attention to the payment platform as both a means of speculation as well as a means of online payment.

Perhaps the easiest way to make money with Bitcoins is by taking a long position on the currency. Though Bitcoin is not stock, it can be viewed as a commodity in its own right. After all, it is bought and sold on a public platform. Nevertheless, it is not treated as such in its marketplace. It is a currency that can be exchanged for with other currencies such as the dollar or Euro. Given this fact, if it is to be believed that Bitcoin will continue to thrive and gain a large following worldwide, the value of the currency will rise over time due to its scarceness. Each and every Bitcoin will be worth more and more as sustained use introduces the currency to new markets who desire a digital method of payment. In this way a long position on the currency could be very lucrative if Bitcoin's value finds a permanent spot in the online payment space. That said, in no way is this an enticement to simply hoard Bitcoins. The prospect of a profitable long position is only made possible by the encouragement of the currency being utilized as it was meant to be utilized, i.e. as a means of online payment. If enough people begin to stockpile the currency in hopes that their Bitcoins will be worth more than they are today, the currency will quickly find its value completely diminished. What gives Bitcoins their desirability is that it is a common currency that can be used all around the world. The currency makes it simple for international transactions and provides individuals with the power to control their transactions instead of banks. Without the correct propagation of the currency, it will gradually cease to be viewed as a store of value as demand whittles itself away. Granted this outcome would require a multitude of people to completely halt the use of the currency as a means of trade, but it is nonetheless possible. Thus, a warning: if you were hoping to snatch up a boatload of Bitcoins and sit on them until their value skyrockets, it won't work unless you contribute to the Bitcoin community and use the currency the way it was intended.

If buying up Bitcoins is not for you, yet another way to invest in Bitcoin is by accepting the currency for any personal business ventures you may be a part of. For instance, if an individual were to run an online stuffed animal business, in lieu of accepting dollars or Yen as payment for goods sold, customers could pay in Bitcoins. This idea works for most any sort of side project as well. Music, eBooks, even if it's a simple blog, you could accept Bitcoin donations for your efforts. By doing so, not only will you be building your own wealth of Bitcoins, but you will be directly contributing to the currency by offering another location for Bitcoin users to make online purchases or donations. This will further bolster the currency and increase its total number of transactions, allowing it to grasp a firmer hold in the online payment space while netting you at least a few more Bitcoins.

What Resources Are Available to Learn More About Bitcoins?

To help with any questions you may have about Bitcoin or for more help on getting started with the currency, below is a list of resources both informational and actionable:

- Informational:
  - http://visual.ly/bitcoin-explained?utm_campaign=website&utm_source=sendgrid
  - http://www.youtube.com/watch?v=CdVVECKKSXo
  - https://www.youtube.com/watch?v=Um63OQz3bjo&feature=player_embedded
  - http://bitcoin.org/en/
  - http://en.wikipedia.org/wiki/Bitcoin
  - https://en.bitcoin.it/wiki/Main_Page
  - https://en.bitcoin.it/wiki/Trade
  - http://bitcoincharts.com/

- http://blockchain.info/charts
- http://bitcoinmagazine.com/
- http://www.bitcoinnews.com/
- https://bitcointalk.org/index.php?board=77.0
- http://bitcoin.org/bitcoin.pdf
- http://www.forbes.com/sites/kashmirhill/2013/05/01/living-on-bitcoin-for-a-week-the-journey-begins/

➢ Actionable:

- http://www.weusecoins.com/en/
- https://play.google.com/store/apps/details?id=de.schildbach.wallet
- https://bitcoinfoundation.org/donate
- https://www.spendbitcoins.com/places/
- https://bitpay.com/featured-merchants
- https://en.bitcoin.it/wiki/Merchant_Howto
- http://btcmerchants.com/
- http://www.coinsetter.com/index.html
- https://www.kraken.com/

The Bitcoinist website is a complete way to stay abreast of the Bitcoin market—visit regularly for the latest news and information on Bitcoins.

www.TheBitcoinist.com

To stay current with the world of bitcoin, please consider the Digital Currency Council, where you can get the latest information and expertise on bitcoin from the leaders in the industry. You can also get certified as an expert in the world of digital currency. For more information, please go to http://www.digitalcurrencycouncil.com/?pa=thebitcoinist

Follow The Bitcoinist on Twitter at www.Twitter.com/Bitcoinist

About the Authors

Ryan Lancelot is a recent graduate of The College of New Jersey. This is his first book. Ryan lives in New Jersey.

Jack Tatar is the author of three books, most recently *Having the Talk: The Four Keys to Your Parents' Safe Retirement*. He's interested in Bitcoins but feels that they are not safe for retirement ... at least not yet.

www.ingramcontent.com/pod-product-compliance
Lightning Source LLC
LaVergne TN
LVHW010943110826
845149LV00013B/2736

* 9 7 8 0 9 8 5 0 8 2 0 6 2 *